RUSSELL HOBAN
THE RAIN DOOR

Illustrated by
QUENTIN BLAKE

LONDON · VICTOR GOLLANCZ LTD · 1986

First published in Great Britain 1986
by Victor Gollancz Ltd,
14 Henrietta Street, London WC2E 8QJ

Text copyright © Russell Hoban 1986
Illustrations copyright © Quentin Blake 1986

British Library Cataloguing in Publication Data

Hoban, Russell
The rain door.
I. Title   II. Blake, Quentin
813′,54[J]   PZ7

ISBN 0-575-03097-6

Printed in Italy
by Imago Publishing Ltd

It was on a Thursday that Harry found the rain door. It was a hot summer Thursday and the London streets were glaring in the sunlight. People in the parks and commons took off most of their clothes and lay baking on the grass. People in shops and offices moved slowly in the shade of blinds and awnings. Dogs panted, cats lay with closed eyes.

The rag-and-bone man went by with his horse and wagon. On the wagon were an old iron water tank and a jumble of lead and copper pipes.

Harry never could be sure of what it was the rag-and-bone man shouted: Any lumber up? Any jumble up?

Harry stuck his head out of the window. "What did you say?" he shouted to the rag-and-bone man.

"Rainy numbers up," shouted the rag-and-bone man.

"What rainy numbers?" Harry shouted back.

"Any thunder up?" shouted the rag-and-bone man.

"Gee-up, Lightning," he said quietly to his horse, and off they went.

Harry went after them but when he came out of the house they were nowhere to be seen. Harry looked up and down the road. He saw a shining, it looked like wetness, it looked like water.

"That must be where the rainy numbers come up," said Harry. He went towards the wetness. When he got there it was gone. On one side was the terrace where Harry lived. On the other side was the common. There was shade from the trees on the edge of the common. Harry looked into the shade.

"Rainy numbers up," he said. He looked up but then he was looking through the shade into the sunlight on the other side of it. Harry looked down and away. While his head was bent down he looked back into the shade out of the corner of one eye. He saw something flickering.

"Rainy numbers," said Harry. They didn't look like ordinary numbers, they were strange shapes. He wondered if there might be a door anywhere.

Harry looked for a knocker. There was no knocker. He looked for a letterbox. There was no letterbox. There was no door knob or handle. Harry looked for a keyhole. When he found it he put his mouth to it and said, "How do I get in?"

A voice said, "Who is it?"
Harry said, "It's Harry."
"What do you want?" said the voice.
"Rain," said Harry.
"And very reasonable too," said the voice. "Only
it's the line, you see. You'll have to draw it off."
"I'll bring a pencil," said Harry.
"Not that kind of a line," said the voice.
"It's the roaring kind."
"Lion!" said Harry.
"That's what I said," said the voice. "He's much
too close, you see. He's frightening my horse and
I can't get these hoses screwed together."
Then Harry knew whose voice it was. "You'll have
to open the door for me," he said.
"You'll have to say the right words," said
the voice. "And this is the rain door, you know.
Once you're in you won't get out till rain time."
"I'll have a go," said Harry.

The door opened. Harry had thought that the rag-and-bone man would
be just on the other side of it but he wasn't.
There was a long hot dry and stony valley under a hot desert sun.
Far away at the end of the valley was a mountain with a dark cloud on
the top of it.
But there was no rag-and-bone man in sight.
"Where are you?" shouted Harry. No answer.
"Hello!" shouted Harry. "Mr Rag-and-Bone!"
Still no answer. Harry looked behind him for the door he had come in
by but there was no door. There was nothing but a stony desert all
round and the heat waves dancing on the rocks. Far off he heard a
lion roar.
"I don't want to play this any more," said Harry. "I want to go home."
But he couldn't see any way of getting home.
The lion roared and Harry could hear the neighing of a horse.

"It's not coming any closer," said Harry. "If I just stay here maybe I'll be all right." But then he thought of the rag-and-bone man and his frightened horse. "I'll go just a little closer and see what I can see," said Harry. He kept his eyes open for weapons. He thought he might see a magic sword stuck in a rock or perhaps a magic ring lying about. But he didn't see any swords or rings. Harry kept going towards the lion's roar. He saw all kinds of things among the rocks.

He saw rags and bones and old iron. He saw string and wire and rope and rusty bolts and thrown-away clocks and an old horn. He saw hammers and drills and pliers and tongs. It was the rag-and-bone man's scrap yard. It was the bones that gave Harry an idea. They were enormous bones, they must have come from dinosaurs.
"Probably a dinosaur would frighten the lion," said Harry.

He quickly set to work to make one.
   He used bones and rags and iron and rope,
            he used wire and rusty bolts.

He used gears and wheels and mainsprings
      from all the old clocks he could find.

When the dinosaur was all put together
it had keys all over it for winding
up the different parts of it.

It had a steering wheel to steer it with
and it had a horn that went,
GAHOOGA.

Harry wound up all the different parts of his dinosaur and off he went to help the rag-and-bone man and his horse. It was hard going because the different parts of the dinosaur all ran down at different times and Harry had to keep jumping off to wind them up. But the dinosaur took giant steps and it moved fast.

Soon Harry got to the end of the valley. There he saw the lion prowling round the rag-and-bone man's wagon. The rag-and-bone man was in a tangle of old garden hoses and crusted pipes. He was keeping the lion off with a length of pipe while the horse plunged and kicked and the wagon bounced and rattled.

Harry sounded his horn, GAHOOGA! The lion laid his ears back and crouched down. Harry wound up all his clockwork and the dinosaur stomped towards the lion. GAHOOGA! went the horn. The lion slunk away lashing its tail.

"Thank you for seeing off the lion," said the rag-and-bone man. "But now you're frightening Lightning with your dinosaur."

"If I send the dinosaur away we'll probably have that lion after us again," said Harry.

"That's all right," said the rag-and-bone man. "Thunder after Lightning is as it should be. It's only when he thunders out of turn that he makes her nervous."

Harry wound up all the dinosaur's clockwork and sent it stomping back to the scrap yard.

"We'd best get moving," said the rag-and-bone man.
"Here," he said to Harry, "you take the reins."

"Gee-up, Lightning," said Harry. As the wagon jolted along the
rag-and-bone man screwed together pieces of old hose which he paid
out behind them. The pieced-together hose stretched out down the
valley, up the mountain side, and into the dark cloud on top of the
mountain.
"What's up there on top of the mountain?" Harry asked the rag-and-bone man.
"It's an old iron water tank I use for a cloud-catcher," said the
rag-and-bone man. "Here comes the lion again."

"Gee-up!" said Harry to Lightning. Lightning broke into a gallop and the wagon rattled through the valley with the lion thundering after it. "Faster!" said the rag-and-bone man. He was screwing a pipe on to the end of the hose. On the end of the pipe was an enormous battered old sprinkler head.

BANG! Lightning crashed into the rain door and they burst through.
They were not down on the common where Harry had first gone through the
rain door, they were high in the sky over London. Lightning was galloping
faster, the wagon was rattling and rumbling, the lion was thundering close
behind them, he was booming and roaring till the whole sky echoed with it.
The rag-and-bone man opened the rain valve and the rain poured down.

Round and round they rattled and roared, rolling on the rain road high
in the sky, raining down on London. Harry drove furiously, Lightning
galloped faster and faster, the wet and shining lion roared his thunder
through the rain.

When the rain had settled down to a steady downpour the rag-and-bone
man closed the rain valve, unscrewed the pipe with the sprinkler
head, and threw the hose off the back of the wagon. "I'll roll it up
later," he said. "The rain will carry on by itself now, and we can call it a
day. Bring her down, Harry, and I'll drop you off."
Harry reined Lightning in. "Easy, old girl," he said, "easy does it."
He swung the wagon low over the common and rattled gently down in
front of his house.

"Thanks for letting me drive your wagon," he said to the rag-and-bone man.
"Thanks for helping me out," said the rag-and-bone man. "See you."
"See you," said Harry.
"Any old thunder!" shouted the rag-and-bone man as he drove off.
Lightning nickered, and high over the common the thunder rolled far away.
"Gahooga," said Harry, and went into the house.